LIVRONS-NOUS

An Art Installation that Won the Prix du Public award in Montpellier, France

A thirty-foot-high testament to the enduring power of books and writing.

Photo credit: Photoarchitecture

Continued on Pg. 8

Editor's Note

Dear Readers,

As we launch the 45th edition of VMH Magazine, I am humbled and thrilled to share this momentous milestone with each and every one of you. This edition holds a special place in our hearts as we continue to build upon the legacy of quality content, thought-provoking insights, and uplifting stories that have defined VMH Magazine over the years.

Amidst the bustle of our daily lives, it is crucial that we take the time to pause, reflect, and check in with ourselves. The importance of constantly ensuring our own well-being cannot be overstated. It is a testament to our resilience and strength to acknowledge when we need to lighten our load, seek support, and nurture our minds and bodies. We must remember that being okay is not merely a destination but an ongoing journey that requires mindfulness and self-compassion.

In this edition, we delve into the theme of self-recognition and personal breakthroughs. "You Are Your Breakthrough" encapsulates the spirit of empowering oneself to fulfill dreams, overcome challenges, and recognize the power within. We explore the impact of nurturing our moral compass in a digital age, emphasizing the values that guide our interactions and decisions in an increasingly interconnected world.

Our journey then takes us to France, where we celebrate the art installation "Livrons-nous," winner of the prestigious Prix du Public award. The convergence of art and public acclaim exemplifies the enduring influence of creativity and expression in our lives, inspiring us to seek beauty and meaning in every corner of the world.

Furthermore, we explore the evolving role of artificial intelligence in counseling, understanding that while AI can offer valuable support, human empathy and connection remain irreplaceable. This nuanced discussion reinforces the significance of preserving the human touch in our pursuit of progress and innovation.

As we navigate these diverse and compelling topics, it is essential to remember that our well-being, aspirations, and fulfillment are intertwined. We deserve happiness, respect for our talents, fair financial compensation, and above all, dignity and respect in our personal and professional endeavors. These principles underpin the essence of our publication and guide the stories we champion and elevate.

I extend my deepest gratitude to our readers whose unwavering support has propelled VMH Magazine to new heights. Together, we continue to foster a community that champions positivity, and embraces the journey of self-discovery.

Thank you for embarking on this enriching journey with us.

Vikki Jones
Editor-in-Chief

Table of Contents

Cover Image: Vikki Jones
Photography Credit: Vikki Jones

5 WAYS TO MAKE THE MOST OF YOUR MONEY

FAMILY FEATURES

Working toward financial stability can be a daunting task, but developing healthy spending habits and practicing smart saving can make it easier to plan for the future and take control of your finances.

Improve your financial stability and security with these tips from the experts at Credit One Bank, a data-driven financial services company that is also one of the largest and fastest-growing credit card issuers in the United States.

Create a Spending Plan and Budget

By building a budget and examining your spending habits, you're able to see exactly how much money you have coming in and where – or on what – you're spending it. This is often the first step toward meeting short- and long-term financial goals, whether those involve taking a vacation, paying off debt, buying a new house or saving for retirement.

Add up your household income, including paychecks and other income, such as investments or rental property, then figure your monthly expenses starting with recurring bills like rent or mortgage, car payments, insurance, utilities and subscriptions. Also account for variable expenses like gas, groceries and entertainment. Once you have your income and expenses calculated, look for places you may be able to cut back to help meet your financial goals. Don't forget to be flexible; your budget and spending will change along with your needs and situation.

Earn Rewards on Everyday Purchases

You can stretch your budget further by taking advantage of rewards offered by your bank or credit card company. For example, some credit cards provide cash back rewards for

specific everyday purchases. An option like the Credit One Bank Platinum Rewards Visa is one such credit card. Customers can earn 5% cash back for the first $5,000 of eligible purchases per year on things like gas, groceries, internet, cable, satellite TV and mobile phone services, plus 1% cash back rewards on all other purchases.

"Make sure your rewards are working for you – and not just as a gimmicky signup bonus," said David Herpers, head of product at Credit One Bank. "Find a credit card that continues to give you more for your everyday spending habits."

Compare Interest Rates When Opening a Savings Account

When selecting a savings account, look for the highest yield but also consider the minimum balance requirement, any introductory rates that may expire after a set period of time and the ease with which you're able to access your money and account information. Often, digital banks can offer higher rates than traditional brick-and-mortar branches due to their lower overhead costs. Ensure any bank you consider is a member of the Federal Deposit Insurance Corporation (FDIC) so you can earn a fair rate and protect your money.

Build an Emergency Fund

Emergency funds create a financial buffer that can keep you afloat in times of need without having to rely on high-interest loans or maxing out a line of credit. These funds can be used to pay for large, unexpected expenses such as medical bills, the loss of a job, car repairs or home appliance repair or replacement.

To build your emergency fund, set a monthly savings goal - even an amount as small as $50 per paycheck can make an impact over time - and set up a way for the funds to be automatically transferred to the account each time you get paid to make the task less daunting. Check on the account periodically and adjust if necessary or if your budget allows. A good rule of thumb is to set aside 3-6 months of living expenses.

Keep Track of Your Credit

Your credit score provides lenders and other parties a quick way to get an idea of your financial history and your ability to pay. Having a good credit score typically provides better interest rates and makes it easier to get approval on loans, rent an apartment, take out a mortgage or finance large purchases. Poor credit can saddle you with higher rates and lead to potential loan requests being denied.

To help you understand how different actions affect your credit score, many sites offer free credit reports and tools that allow you to stay up-to-date and track your score over time. Be sure to check reviews and verify the site's legitimacy before entering your information. Additionally, many credit card companies, including Credit One Bank, provide free access to online credit reports on a regular basis to give customers an easier way to stay on top of their finances.

Find more ways to make your money work for you at CreditOneBank.com/articles.

Understanding Emerging Card Capabilities

Alternative methods of payment, like credit and debit cards, have now been around for decades and have grown in popularity due to their convenience in comparison to cash, but technology has evolved even further to allow for a rise in contactless payment. Consider these capabilities many cards now offer:

Chip (EMV) cards utilize smart technology to store data on the microchip embedded in the card, allowing for an extra level of security with a one-time code generated as part of each transaction to keep

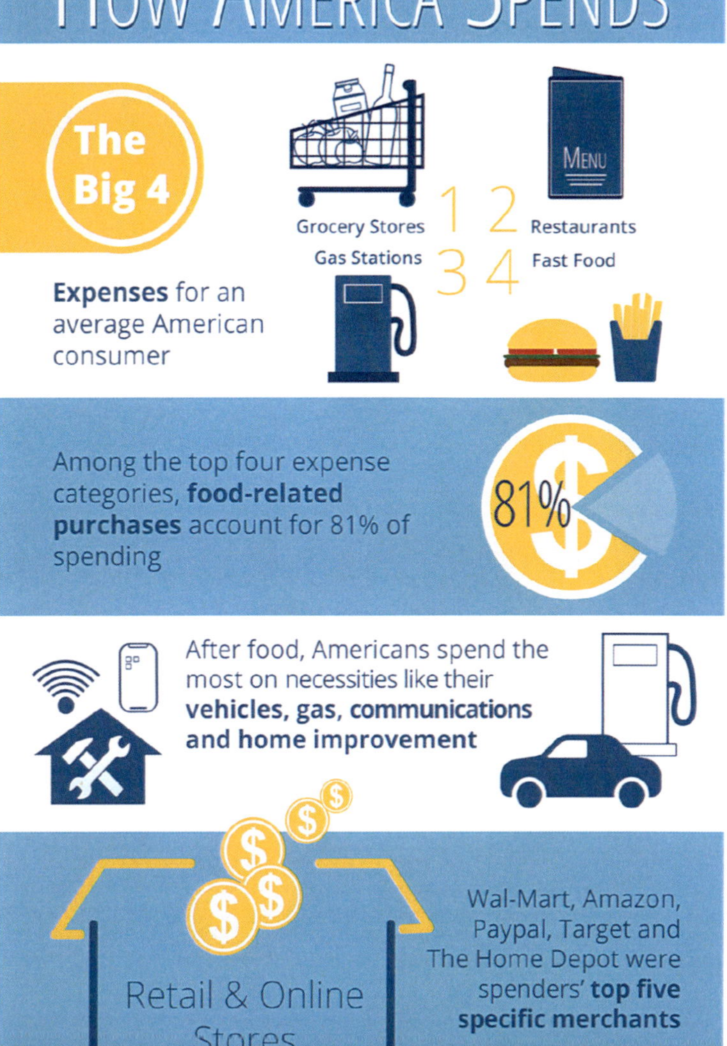

payment information more secure than swiping the magnetic strip.

Contactless cards are equipped with near-field communication technology that allows payments to be made at a terminal without swiping or inserting. The card member's name, billing information and security code are never transmitted when cards bearing the contactless indicator are tapped on an equipped terminal.

Smart device payments can be made by adding your credit or debit card to the wallet app on your smartphone or tablet. Apps can also be added to some smartwatches to make contactless payments at participating merchants even easier.

Photo courtesy of Getty Images (man and woman with computer)

Camille Maire, Viviane Le Deunff, and Charlotte Jeanjean, three talented architects and friends inspired by various realms, have achieved a remarkable feat with their art installation "Livrons-nous," which garnered the prestigious Prix du Public award at the Festival des Architectures Vives in Montpellier, France. This monumental creation captivates audiences with its thought-provoking and poetic examination of the sanctity of the world and its evolution.

Set within the historic courtyard of the Ginestous private hotel, "Livrons-nous" stands proudly as a thirty-foot-high testament to the enduring power of books and writing. Its enchanting form takes shape as a towering spiral, composed of a thousand loose pages gracefully escaping from an ancient, majestic book, and ascending toward the heavens. This captivating display invites visitors to immerse themselves in

Photo credits: Photoarchitecture

"LIVRONS-NOUS" EXPANSIVE REACH EXTENDS BEYOND THE HISTORIC COURTYARD, PROMISING THE POTENTIAL FOR ADAPTATION TO VARIOUS SPACES.

the evocative world of literature, offering a respite from the frenetic pace of the digital era and fostering moments of contemplation and wonder.

As spectators witness the pages of the installation whimsically drifting upwards, they are encouraged to unleash their creativity and imagination at a vintage school desk, symbolizing a nostalgic return to the innocence of childhood. "Livrons-nous" serves as a gateway to the imaginary realm of storytelling, inviting individuals to reconnect with the timeless allure of literature and indulge in the pleasures of daydreaming.

Moreover, this awe-inspiring creation not only pays homage to the written word but also unlocks the hitherto inaccessible courtyard of the Ginestous hotel, establishing a harmonious interplay between the venerable stones of the 13th-century edifice and the contemporary artistic installation. With its colorimetric and sensory resonance, "Livrons-nous" seamlessly bridges the gap between the ancient and the modern, breathing new life into the historic space.

The team behind this extraordinary endeavor comprises three accomplished architects, each bringing their unique expertise to the project. Camille Maire, known for her prowess in rehabilitation projects and her commitment to sustainable design, leads the charge alongside Viviane Le Deunff, whose passion for architectural practice and artistic research enriches the installation with depth and vibrancy. Completing the trio is Charlotte Jeanjean, an architect and energy auditor with a penchant for enhancing housing energy performance, who brings her invaluable insights to the project.

Through their artful vision and collaborative spirit, Camille Maire, Viviane Le Deunff, and Charlotte Jeanjean have breathed life into "Livrons-nous," a mesmerizing ode to the enduring legacy of the written word and a celebration of the boundless imagination it inspires. This triumphant installation serves as a testament to the profound impact of art in transcending time and space, leaving an indelible mark on all who encounter its enchanting splendor.

Photo credis: Photoarchitecture

Release Your Greatness

Written by Vikki Jones

In a world filled with immense possibilities and endless opportunities, it is disheartening to witness countless individuals holding themselves back from realizing their full potential. Far too often, self-doubt and fear of failure prevent us from taking that leap of faith and embracing our greatness. But what if, just for a moment, we set aside our doubts and allowed ourselves to truly explore our strengths, talents, and unique abilities? What if we dared to think outside of the box and invested in our belief in ourselves? The results could be nothing short of extraordinary.

Each one of us possesses an incredible reservoir of untapped potential. However, it is only by giving ourselves a chance that we can unlock this hidden greatness. It begins with a journey inward, a sincere examination of our strengths and talents. By identifying and developing these strong points, we lay the foundation for our success.

Think of yourself as a diamond in the rough. You have the potential to shine brilliantly, but it requires effort, patience, and a willingness to invest in self-improvement. Take the time to discover what truly brings you joy and fulfillment. Nurture those passions and talents, for they are the keys to unlocking your greatness.

It is also crucial to break free from the confines of conventional thinking. The world is changing rapidly, and the most successful individuals are those who can adapt and think outside of the box.

Embrace innovation, challenge the status quo, and be unafraid to take calculated risks. By doing so, you open up a world of possibilities and pave the way for greatness to flow into your life.

However, none of this is possible without a strong belief in oneself. Confidence is the driving force behind every successful person. Believe in your abilities, your dreams, and your potential. Surround yourself with positive influences, seek out mentors who can guide you, and never underestimate the power of self-affirmation.

It is important to recognize that greatness does not come easily or overnight. It is a journey, filled with obstacles and setbacks. But it is through these challenges that we grow, learn, and become stronger. Embrace failure as a stepping stone to success and never let setbacks deter you from pursuing your dreams.

So, I implore you to give yourself a chance. Look deep within, develop your strong points, and allow yourself the opportunity to think outside of the box. Invest in and strengthen your belief in yourself. Know that you have what it takes to be great. Believe it, embrace it, and watch as your greatness flows effortlessly into every aspect of your life.

CES Great Minds, The State of Streaming, Byron Allen

CTA Executive with L'oreal Group Photo at CES L'oreal Keynote

Hisense VP David Gold Speaking Speaking at CES Hisense Press Conference

Las Vegas Aces President Nikki Fargas | Photo Credit: Vikki Jones

Hyundai Media taking picture at CES Hyundai Press Conference

UNVEILING THE FUTURE OF TECH AND INNOVATION
CES 2024

Photo Credits: Consumer Technology Association

The Consumer Electronics Show (CES) 2024 in Las Vegas marked the beginning of a groundbreaking year in technology, hosting an array of 4300+ exhibitors, including 1400+ startups, and welcoming a record 135,000+ attendees from over 150 countries. With an impressive 2.5+ million net square feet of exhibits, it remains the dominant event across AI, accessibility, digital health, mobility, and much more.

Gary Shapiro, president and CEO of the Consumer Technology Association (CTA)®, emphasized the importance of face-to-face interaction in the technology industry and noted the diversity exhibited, proving that every company must become a tech company. Notably, 60% of Fortune 500 companies were in attendance, solidifying CES as a cornerstone for tech innovation.

CES 2024 emerged as a center for global collaboration and partnership with a focus on solving pressing global challenges. Innovation in AI led the discussions, showcasing how technology is poised to transform communication, business, and care. This event also established access to technology as an essential pillar of the Human Security for All (HS4A) global campaign, promoting the role of tech in enhancing the human experience.

The conference hosted keynotes from prominent figures representing various industries, including a first-time keynote from L'Oréal Groupe, highlighting inclusive beauty tech. Additionally, sustainability took center stage with numerous exhibitors showcasing their commitment to eco-friendly solutions, addressing energy efficiency, renewable sources, and emission reduction.

"The resurgence of CES proves that face-to-face conversations and meetings are a necessity for the technology industry," said Gary Shapiro, president and CEO, Consumer Technology Association (CTA)®. *"For more than 20 years, I've said that every company must become a tech company, and the diversity of exhibitors at CES 2024 proves it. The CES footprint and conference programming span the entire tech ecosystem."*

The Digital Health Summit brought attention to tools and technologies aiming to improve health equity and lower healthcare costs. Mark Cuban and his Cost Plus Drug Company unveiled a new partnership, emphasizing the role of technology in healthcare advancements.

C Space featured conversations on tech trends affecting content consumption, AI, programmatic and connected TV, and advertising. Gaming and E-Sports were also in the limelight, with advancements in inclusivity and accessibility shaping the entertainment landscape.

CES 2024 was not just a platform for innovation but also a celebration of CTA's 100th anniversary, symbolizing a century of driving innovation-friendly policies, setting industry standards, and empowering innovators to address global challenges. CES 2024 served as a testament to the ever-evolving tech landscape, setting the stage for the year ahead with its innovative trends, global collaborations, and visionary partnerships.

CTA President and CEO Gary Shapiro Speaking at Siemens CES Keynote

CES Walmart Keynote Audiences

Adena Friedman, NASDAQ CEO

YOU ARE YOUR BREAKTHROUGH

In life and business, it's easy to overlook the power and influence we possess. The daily grind, challenges, and never-ending to-do lists often distract us from realizing the magnitude of our own strength. But it's important to take a step back and acknowledge the progress we've made. Each step forward, no matter how small, has led to where we are today. It's crucial to recognize that the key to fulfilling our aspirations lies within us.

As we reflect on our journey, from sleepless nights to relentless pursuit of our goals, it becomes evident that we possess the fortitude and creativity to overcome challenges and make a difference. We have the ability to shape our own destiny and influence the world around us. It's a matter of tapping into our potential, understanding our capabilities, and recognizing that the breakthrough we seek is within ourselves. We are the driving force behind our successes and have the power to continue creating impact. The connections we form and the experiences we accumulate along the way only serve to reinforce this notion. As we expand our network and encounter new opportunities, it's essential to remember that the ultimate power lies within us. Our talents, passion, and drive are the fuel that propels us forward.

Photo: Vikki Jones, Owner VMH Publishing, VMH Magazine & VMH Sports Magazine | Photo Credit: Vikki Jones

We are the driving force behind our successes and have the power to continue creating impact. The connections we form and the experiences we accumulate along the way only serve to reinforce this notion. As we expand our network and encounter new opportunities, it's essential to remember that the ultimate power lies within us. Our talents, passion, and drive are the fuel that propels us forward.

The realization that we are the breakthrough we've been searching for can be both empowering and humbling. We are the key to fulfilling our needs and desires. What has brought us to this point will carry us forward. Despite challenges and doubts, our inner strength remains unwavering. This understanding propels us forward, guiding our path and inspiring those around us.

"KEEP DOING WHAT YOU'RE DOING. YOU ARE YOUR BREAKTHROUGH. THOSE ATTRIBUTES ABOUT YOU THAT GOT YOU HERE WILL GET YOU TO YOUR DESTINATION. BELIEVE IN YOURSELF AND YOUR ABILITIES, AND KEEP MOVING FORWARD. YOUR BREAKTHROUGH IS WITHIN REACH, AND IT'S UP TO YOU TO MAKE IT HAPPEN."

Recognize the strength within yourself and the impact you have on the world. Take the time to reflect on your journey and realize that the answer to your breakthrough lies within. You possess the power to shape your destiny and influence the world around you. Embrace your potential and unleash the breakthrough from within.

How to Recognize Your Impact and Your Potential:

1. Reflect on Your Achievements: Take time to reflect on your journey and the successes you have achieved. Recognize the role you played in overcoming challenges and making progress.

2. Understand Your Value: Identify the unique strengths, talents, and skills that have contributed to your achievements. Acknowledge the impact that your capabilities have had on your journey.

3. Embrace Your Network: Recognize the value of the connections you have formed and the experiences you have gained. Understand how these relationships have influenced your growth and reinforced your abilities.

4. Seek New Opportunities: As you expand your network and encounter new opportunities, remain open to the possibilities they present. Understand that the ultimate power to seize these opportunities lies within you.

5. Pursue Your Passions: Embrace your talents, passion, and drive as the driving force behind your accomplishments. Recognize that these qualities are the fuel propelling you forward towards further success.

6. Trust in Your Potential: Believe in your own capacity to create impact and influence the world around you. Understand that the breakthrough you seek comes from within you, and trust in your ability to bring about positive change.

The Home Depot Foundation Invests $6 Million in Skilled Trades Training - New Scholarship and Entrepreneurship Partnerships

The Home Depot Foundation announced an incremental investment of more than $6 millionin skilled trades training and launched new strategic partnerships to address the nearly 400,000 job openings across the construction industry. With these philanthropic grants, the *Foundation's Path to Pro program* launched a brand new entrepreneurship program and will provide free, skilled trades training and scholarships for more veterans, military families, high school students and separating service members.

To serve aspiring entrepreneurs within the skilled trades industry, The Home Depot Foundation is partnering with Bunker Labs to introduce an entrepreneurship program designed to guide U.S. military veterans and military spouses through the process of establishing a successful business foundation. During the 8-week program, participants will gain industry-specific mentorship, learn about market segmentation, how to address specific customer profiles and design a business plan for launch. The program's virtual offering makes it accessible to participants nationwide.

The Foundation is also expanding its Path to Pro scholarship program with grants to SkillPointe Foundation, its partner since 2021, and through a new partnership with Folds of Honor. Military scholarships through Folds of Honor extend financial support to qualifying veterans and military family members entering or enrolled in accredited skilled trade schools.

"We're expanding our current training programs and creating new avenues to steadily fill the country's skilled labor gap with in-demand talent," said The Home Depot Foundation's executive director, Shannon Gerber. "Diversifying our approach with additional entrepreneurship and scholarship programs helps ensure we're reaching more communities with free training opportunities and creating sustainable change for the industry."

The Home Depot Foundation extended its grant to long-time partner Home Builders Institute to broaden its Path to Pro high school and military programs. The two organizations will continue to provide no-cost PACT curriculum certification for more than 1,200 separating military members annually, 11th and 12th grade students and Title 1 schools nationwide.

The Home Depot Foundation's skilled trades training program, Path to Pro, launched in 2018 with a $50 million commitment to train the next generation of skilled tradespeople, diversify the trades industry, and address the growing labor shortage in the U.S. The Foundation's trades-focused partnerships have introduced more than 200,000 people to the skilled trades and have trained more than 41,000 participants through programming available to youth, high school students, underserved communities and separating U.S. military.

Beyond the Foundation's work in this area, The Home Depot's Path to Pro Network connects skilled tradespeople to professional contractors and job openings. *For more information and to find skilled trades resources available in English and Spanish, visit PathtoPro.com.*

NURTURING OUR MORAL COMPASS IN A DIGITAL AGE

---

*PRACTICAL STEPS FOR CULTIVATING
ETHICAL NAVIGATION*

WRITTEN BY VIKKI JONES

Photo Credit: Canva

As human beings, we are born into this world with an inherent conscience, a compass that helps us distinguish right from wrong. As we grow and develop, we refine this inner guide, which becomes our moral compass, steering us through the complexities of life. This essential tool assists us in making thoughtful decisions not only for ourselves but also in understanding their impact on those around us.

When this compass isn't properly honed, moral disorientation can occur. Without a well-trained conscience, individuals may struggle to discern between right and wrong, impacting their own character and influencing others. In today's society, the pervasive influence of superficial visuals and fabricated narratives on social media can distort our understanding of reality. The normalization of degradation and negativity in online content can desensitize individuals, leading them to adopt harmful mindsets and behaviors.

It's crucial to recognize that while technology plays a significant role in shaping our experiences, the responsibility ultimately lies with people, not machines. Thus, it becomes essential for individuals to intentionally cultivate and maintain their moral compass. This act is undeniably challenging, as it involves resisting the allure of immediate desires in favor of making morally guided decisions.

Finding the time for introspection and reflection amidst the fast pace of modern life is pivotal. Embracing moments of solitude and quiet reflection enables individuals to delve within

themselves, align with their moral values, and make decisions they can stand behind. Through this deliberate pause, one can rediscover their moral compass, providing a steady guide in their journey.

Additionally, one's faith and belief system can serve as a robust foundation for maintaining a well-functioning moral compass. Faith and belief offer profound wisdom, establish healthy boundaries, and provide ethical guidance, surpassing conventional approaches to decision-making. These principles allow individuals to navigate the complexities of life with clarity and purpose.

Despite the pervasive influence of misleading narratives and false portrayals in the digital realm, it is possible to navigate these challenges and shape our lives consciously. By leveraging the tools of self-reflection, faith, and intentional decision-making, individuals can empower themselves to discern truth from fabrication, chart their own course, and embrace meaningful change.

Practical Steps for Cultivating a Moral Compass:

- Self-Reflection: Taking the time to ponder and make decisions we feel good about
- Slowing down and cutting out the noise, allowing ourselves to reflect and develop our moral values
- Seeking moments of solitude to rediscover and realign with our moral compass
- Embracing one's faith and belief system to provide ethical guidance and wisdom

TikTok: Growing Businesses

Written by Vikki Jones

The Most Trendy Fun Ways to Get Your Message Out and Achieve Viral Success

TikTok has taken the world by storm, capturing the attention of millions with its addictive short-form videos. From dance challenges to lip-syncing and DIY hacks, this rapidly growing social media platform has become a hub for creativity and self-expression. However, TikTok isn't just about fun and entertainment; *it has also become a launchpad for individuals to share their messages, grow a global following, and transform their lives.* In this article, we will explore some of the trendiest and most effective ways to use TikTok to get your message out, highlighting success stories of individuals who have gone viral, gained a massive following, and turned their dreams into reality.

1. Engaging Storytelling:
TikTok offers a unique opportunity to captivate audiences through short, visually compelling videos. By harnessing the power of storytelling, individuals can share their experiences, passions, and messages in an engaging way. Whether it's through personal anecdotes, motivational monologues, or relatable content, TikTok users have successfully built a loyal following by connecting with viewers on a deeper level.

2. Educational Content:
TikTok isn't just about entertainment; it also serves as a platform for educating and informing viewers. By creating content that imparts valuable knowledge, individuals can position themselves as experts in their respective fields. Whether it's providing tips and tricks, sharing life hacks, or offering insightful advice, TikTok users have successfully built a dedicated following eager to learn from their expertise.

Success Stories:

TikTok has been a catalyst for numerous success stories, with individuals going from relative obscurity to global fame and fulfilling careers. Take, for example, Charli D'Amelio, who gained a massive following through her captivating dance routines. With over 100 million followers, she has secured brand deals, launched her merchandise, and even starred in music videos, turning her passion for dance into a lucrative profession.

Similarly, Tabitha Brown, a vegan chef, used TikTok to showcase her delicious plant-based recipes and spread positivity. Her infectious personality and cooking skills resonated with millions, leading to a significant increase in her following. Today, she has her own cooking show and has become an influential figure in the vegan community.

TikTok has undoubtedly become a powerful tool for individuals to share their messages, gain global recognition, and turn their dreams into reality. The platform's ability to connect with millions in a short span of time has opened doors for individuals from all walks of life, proving that TikTok is not just a platform for entertainment but a gateway to living one's dreams.

AN INTERVIEW WITH OWNER OF 'S'TITCHES GLAM EXPERIENCE"

TIANA WALKER

Written By: Vikki Jones

Tiana Walker, the Founder and CEO of Stitches Glam Experience, opens up about the driving force behind her success – her unwavering faith in God. Her journey from a young girl styling dolls' hair on the porch to becoming a renowned hairstylist and makeup artist is laced with faith, determination, and a commitment to serving others. In a candid conversation, Tiana shares her profound connection to God and how it intertwines with every aspect of her business and personal life.

"As a stylist, it is so important that you know your audience and how to make their experience with you more personable," Tiana emphasizes. This understanding shapes her approach to her craft, creating a space where clients not only receive exceptional beauty services but also find solace and empowerment.

Tiana's unyielding devotion to her faith shines through as she describes the integral role of God in her professional journey. "I have a true relationship with GOD, and I always follow Him. Everything I do, every choice, decision, and idea goes through Him," she shares.

It is evident that Tiana's business, Stitches Glam Experience, is not just a salon; it is a testament to her deep-rooted conviction in divine guidance and purpose.

The foundation of Tiana's success is built upon principles of character and integrity. "Presentation and Appearance are very important. However, one thing that is as equally important to the other two is 'Character'. Your character, which boils down to your heart, must first be right. Once your heart is in complete alignment with GOD, that steers your presentation and appearance."s he notes. This emphasis on character, rooted in her faith, forms the cornerstone of her brand and influences every interaction with clients.

Tiana's innovative approach to hair styling, particularly her signature stitch braids, embodies her dedication to mastering her craft. "My stitch braids are a technique I studied and didn't take on this title until I knew for sure I mastered my ability to serve this style confidently," she explains. This commitment to excellence, guided by her faith, has garnered the trust and loyalty of her clients, who recognize the divine inspiration behind her work.

Through her unwavering faith, Tiana has overcome adversities and navigated challenges in both her personal and professional life. "My faith has influenced my commitment and my lifestyle. I strongly believe that in this generation if you don't stand for something, you will fall for anything," she asserts. Tiana's unshakeable resolve to stand with God has propelled her to incredible heights and positioned her as a leader in the beauty industry.

Her humble beginnings and relentless pursuit of her passion have led Tiana to be not only a successful entrepreneur but also a source of inspiration for many. "Many are beautiful and talented, but I am humbly gifted," she acknowledges. It is this humility, coupled with unwavering faith, that sets Tiana apart in her field.

As Stitches Glam Experience continues to flourish, Tiana's faith remains the driving force behind her vision for the future. My footsteps are ordered by Him, and

He is strategically aligning the right people, great opportunities, and sending investors and connections," she affirms. Her journey is a testament to the transformative power of faith, perseverance, and unwavering dedication to her calling.

Tiana Walker's story is a testament to the extraordinary outcomes that result from placing unwavering faith in God at the helm of one's endeavors. Through her journey, she exemplifies how faith and determination can lead to unparalleled success, while remaining grounded in humility and grace.

Stitches Glam Experience stands as a testament to Tiana's unwavering faith and commitment to excellence, providing not only top-quality beauty services but also an atmosphere of inspiration and empowerment for all who walk through its doors.

Visit www.stitchesglamexperience.com to learn more.

My relationship with GOD is my driving force. Honestly I will say this in complete boldness that I would not even consider running a business if I didn't have GOD.

AI Can Support — But Not Replace — Human Counselors, According to New Recommendations

Artificial intelligence (AI) shows promise as a valuable support tool for delivery of mental health services, educational guidance and career counseling. But the American Counseling Association (ACA), the leading organization representing counseling professionals, warns that consumers should not use AI as a substitute for a human counselor.

ACA's AI Working Group has issued a set of guidelines to help counselors and their clients understand the value and limitations of using chatbots, robotics and other nascent AI tools in mental health services. Clients should understand the technical shortcomings, unresolved biases and security risks of AI before using it as part of their counseling, says Russell Fulmer, PhD, LPC, chair of the working group and professor and director of graduate counseling programs at Husson University in Bangor, Maine.

"AI may offer promising benefits, but its claims can sometimes be overly ambitious and simplified, non-evidence based, or even incorrect and potentially harmful," the panel states in its recommendations.

AI technologies are designed to engage in the same reasoning, decision-making and language comprehension of the human mind. Counselors already use them to automate administrative tasks such as reports on a client's progress, says Olivia Uwamahoro Williams, PhD, NCC, LPC, clinical assistant professor of counseling education at the College of William & Mary in Williamsburg, Virginia, and a member of the ACA working group. Some are inviting clients to use AI chatbots to help them understand and manage their thoughts and feelings between therapy sessions, Fulmer says.

But as the ACA panel notes, the algorithms include the same fallibilities and biases of the humans who create them. The AI tools may rely on data that overlook certain communities, particularly marginalized groups, creating the risk of culturally insensitive care. They risk providing false claims or inaccurate information. And although they show promise as a diagnostic aid, they can't replicate the professional reasoning and expertise required to accurately assess an individual's mental health needs.

"Unlike human counselors, AI lacks the ability to holistically consider a client's complex personal history, cultural context, and varied symptoms and factors among others," the guidelines state.

"Therefore, while AI can be a supportive tool, it should not replace the professional judgment of professional counselors. It is recommended that AI be used as an adjunct to, rather than a replacement for, the expertise provided by professional counselors."

The ACA panel recommends that clients consider the following:

- Make sure your provider informs you about what AI can and cannot offer so you can make informed decisions about using it as part of your counseling.
- To protect confidentiality, verify that the AI tools you use comply with federal and state privacy laws and regulations.
- Discuss with your counselor how to mitigate the risks of AI tools providing falsehoods or factual mistakes that could harm your well-being.
- Refrain from using AI for crisis response, and instead use crisis hotlines, emergency services and other forms of assistance from qualified professionals.

Providers should develop a detailed understanding of AI technologies, their applications in counseling services, and their effects on confidentiality and privacy, the working group says. The recommendations call for counselors to receive comprehensive and continuous training in evolving AI applications, says Fulmer, who studies AI in the behavioral sciences.

"We are ethically obliged before we use something to be quite competent in it," he says. "So, one of our recommendations is to simply accumulate more knowledge about AI."

The panel also calls on technology developers to involve clients and counselors in the design of relevant AI tools. Including these users will ensure that AI tools are client-centered and address real-world needs.

ACA is taking a leadership role in ensuring the appropriate use of AI in mental health services, says Shawn Boynes, FASAE, CAE, the organization's chief executive officer.

"The adoption of AI and its impact on mental health is growing exponentially in a variety of ways that we're still trying to understand," Boynes says. "As one of many mental health organizations focused on well-being, we want to lead by offering solutions to help mitigate future concerns."

PROMOTE YOUR BUSINESS, BRAND, OR PRODUCTS WITH US AT VMH MAGAZINE!

Are you looking to reach a wider audience and increase your brand visibility? Look no further than VMH Magazine, where we provide various packages to help you showcase your business and products effectively.

Benefits of Advertising with VMH Magazine:

- Reach a diverse and engaged audience of readers
- Increase brand awareness and recognition
- Feature your products in a reputable publication
- Tailored advertising packages to suit your needs
- Access to multiple platforms for maximum exposure

Don't miss the opportunity to elevate your business with VMH Magazine. Contact us today to discuss our advertising packages and take your brand to new heights!

www.vmhmagazine.com

CHAZ MD
REVIVING SOULFUL MUSIC AND UPHOLDING ARTISTIC INTEGRITY

Written by Vikki Jones

'MY JEWEL' TOPPING THE INDEPENDENT AIRPLAY CHART, IS A TESTAMENT TO CHAZ MD'S TALENT AND HARD WORK.

"IF YOU COME TO MY SHOW, YOU'RE GOING TO EXPERIENCE GREATNESS, HISTORY IN THE MAKING."

In a world where music often glorifies violence and negativity, artist Chaz MD is a breath of fresh air. In our recent interview with him, he spoke passionately about creating, writing, and singing music that is not nonviolent but good listening. His commitment to providing quality, uplifting music is truly inspiring.

Chaz MD also shed light on the business side of the music industry, particularly the issue of streaming profits. With a growing organic fan base, he has taken control of his music sales by selling directly from his website. This approach not only allows him to connect with his fans on a personal level but also ensures that he receives fair compensation for his art.

Opening up for shows with famed comedian Torry and having his album, 'My Jewel' ranked top on the independent airplay chart, Chaz MD is making waves in the music industry. His dedication to his craft and his refusal to compromise on the quality of his music is truly admirable.

In a world where instant gratification and free access to music are the norm, Chaz MD's stance on the importance of supporting artists by purchasing their music is a powerful reminder. As he aptly put it, "People don't go in the store and buy a drink without paying for it. You should pay for all artists' music and their content so that they can continue doing what they do to bring you that good entertainment that you like."

CHAZ MD PHOTOGRPAHED BY: HITE PHOTOGRAPHY,LLC

CHAZ MD PHOTOGRPAHED BY: HITE PHOTOGRAPHY,LLC

Chaz MD's commitment to delivering the best show possible is evident in his words, "If you come to my show, you're going to experience greatness, history in the making." His passion for his art and his dedication to his fans are truly commendable.

Chaz MD's quotes reflect a deep understanding of the challenges faced by artists in the modern music industry. His unwavering commitment to creating music that is not only a pleasure to listen to but also free from violence and negativity is a testament to his integrity as an artist. In a world where many artists may compromise their values for commercial success, Chaz MD's steadfast dedication to uplifting and nonviolent music is truly refreshing.

The issue of streaming profits is one that plagues many artists in the digital age, and Chaz MD's approach to selling music directly from his website is a bold and empowering move. By taking control of his music sales, he not only ensures fair compensation for his art but also fosters a deeper connection with his fan base. In an industry where artists often struggle to receive their fair share of streaming revenue, Chaz MD's approach is a powerful statement about the importance of valuing and supporting artists' work.

Chaz MD's success in the music industry, from opening up for shows with famed comedian Torry to having his album 'My Jewel' top the independent airplay chart, is a testament to his talent and hard work. His refusal to compromise on the quality of his music and his unwavering commitment to delivering the best show possible have earned him a growing and dedicated fan base.

As we navigate a music industry that can often prioritize commercial success over artistic integrity, Chaz MD's words serve as a powerful reminder of the importance of supporting artists and valuing their work. His call for fans to purchase music and support artists directly highlights the crucial role that fans play in sustaining the careers of their favorite musicians.

In a world where the soul of music often seems to have taken a backseat, Chaz MD's dedication to reviving it is both admirable and inspiring. His commitment to delivering quality, uplifting music and his refusal to compromise on his values are a testament to his integrity as an artist. As he continues to make waves in the music industry, we look forward to seeing him inspire others with his timeless music and unwavering dedication.

COMFORTABLE
CARRYING OPTIONS

Say goodbye to uncomfortable bags. Vikki Jones' designs prioritize comfort, with padded straps, ergonomic handles, and lightweight construction, ensuring a comfortable carrying experience even during long journeys.

Need extra space? Jones' bags feature expandable compartments, allowing you to increase the capacity when needed. Travel with confidence, knowing you have room for souvenirs or extra work documents.

5 HEALTHY HABITS TO HELP REDUCE STRESS

(Family Features) Between work, family obligations and a constantly changing world, people in the United States are stressed. In fact, U.S. workers are among the most stressed in the world, according to a State of the Global Workplace study. While some stress is unavoidable and can be good for you, constant or chronic stress can have real consequences for your mental and physical health.

Chronic stress can increase your lifetime risk of heart disease and stroke. It can also lead to unhealthy habits like overeating, physical inactivity and smoking while also increasing risk factors, including high blood pressure, depression and anxiety. However, a scientific statement from the American Heart Association shows reducing stress and cultivating a positive mindset can improve health and well-being.

To help people understand the connection between stress and physical health, the American Heart Association offers these science-backed insights to help reduce chronic stress.

Stay Active
Exercise is one of the easiest ways to keep your body healthy and release stress. Physical activity is linked to lower risk of diseases, stronger bones and muscles, improved mental health and cognitive function and lower risk of depression. It can also help increase energy and improve quality of sleep. The American Heart Association recommends adults get at least 150 minutes per week of moderate-intensity activity, 75 minutes of vigorous activity or a combination.

Meditate
Incorporate meditation and mindfulness practices into your day to give yourself a few minutes to create some distance from daily stress. Some studies show meditation can reduce blood pressure, improve sleep, support the immune system and increase your ability to process information.

Practice Positivity
A positive mindset can improve overall health. Studies show a positive mindset can help you live longer, and happy individuals tend to sleep better, exercise more, eat better and not smoke. Practice positive self-talk to help you stay calm. Instead of saying, "everything is going wrong," re-frame the situation and remind yourself "I can handle this if I take it one step at a time."

Show Gratitude
Gratitude – or thankfulness – is a powerful tool that can reduce levels of depression and anxiety and improve sleep. Start by simply writing down three things you're grateful for each day.

Find a Furry Friend
Having a pet may help you get more fit; lower stress, blood pressure, cholesterol and blood sugar; and boost overall happiness and well-being. When you see, touch, hear or talk to companion animals, you may feel a sense of goodwill, joy, nurturing and happiness. At the same time, stress hormones are suppressed. Dog ownership is also associated with a lower risk of depression, according to research published by the American Heart Association.

Find more stress-management tips at Heart.org/stress.

Stress 101

Understanding stress is an important step in managing and reducing it. Consider these things to know about stress and how it could affect your life:
- Today, 1 in 3 adults in the U.S. report being worried or depressed.
- Higher levels of the stress hormone cortisol are linked to increased risk of high blood pressure and cardiovascular events like heart disease and stroke.
- The top sources of stress are money, work, family responsibilities and health concerns.
- Work-related stress is associated with a 40% increased risk of cardiovascular disease like heart attack and stroke.

Simone and Tim Harvey (Photo Credit: Vikki Jones)

In a city as diverse as Atlanta, the ability to shift between casual and fine dining experiences, from hole-in-the-wall gems to Michelin-star establishments, is a testament to the thriving culinary scene. New Spot Alert ATL, led by Tim and Simone Harvey, embraces the concept of inclusion, empowering individuals to enhance their atmosphere, expand their palate, and indulge in a variety of gastronomic delights. However, their mission extends far beyond the realm of dining, as they also showcase diverse consumer services, such as beauty and grooming, and celebrate small businesses.

Tim Harvey reflects on the humble origins of New Spot Alert ATL, saying, "We started out by simply going out to eat and

Tim Harvey Prepping for New Spot Alert ATL Showcase

visiting various places for entertainment and services. We realized that if a place was truly exceptional, why not share it with others? Atlanta attracts people from all walks of life, so we decided to create a platform where we could provide recommendations to a wider audience. It has been an incredibly enjoyable journey for us."

Simone Harvey echoes her husband's sentiment, emphasizing the inclusive nature of their platform, "Just as my husband mentioned, it all started with us going out to eat and posting about it on Facebook, tagging ourselves. Soon enough, we received countless calls from people asking for recommendations when they were visiting Atlanta. That's when we decided to create a dedicated platform for everyone to follow, so they can stay updated with our daily recommendations. When you're coming to the Atlanta Metro area, or any area we visit, just head to our Instagram page, 'New Spot Alert ATL.' There, you'll find a diverse range of recommended restaurants to choose from. And what excites me the most is the quality of services that come with these recommendations."

The beauty of New Spot Alert ATL lies not only in its culinary expertise but also in its celebration of the broader business community.

Tim and Simone Harvey understand the significance of showcasing small businesses, recognizing the unique offerings they bring to the table. By highlighting beauty, grooming, and other consumer services, they not only diversify Atlanta's social landscape but also support the entrepreneurs behind these ventures.

Through New Spot Alert ATL, individuals and tourists can enrich their experiences by venturing outside their comfort zones. The platform acts as a guiding light, illuminating a path that leads to unforgettable memories and remarkable discoveries. Whether it's a cozy neighborhood café, a high-end dining establishment, or a hidden gem tucked away in the city, Tim and Simone Harvey's recommendations promise exceptional service and unforgettable experiences.

So, as you plan your next outing or visit to Atlanta, remember to follow @newspotalertatl on Instagram, TikTok, and other social media platforms.

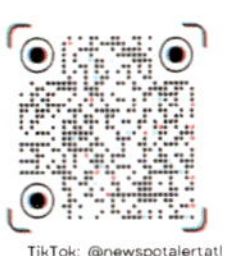

Tim & Simone Harvey Enjoying a New Spot Alert ATL Showcase

ARE READY TO WRITE YOUR BOOK

WRITING A BOOK IS A TRANSFORMATIVE ENDEAVOR THAT CAN OPEN DOORS TO A MULTITUDE OF NEW BUSINESS OPPORTUNITIES.

The world of literature is a vast and captivating realm that allows authors to share their unique perspectives, stories, and knowledge with readers across the globe. If you've ever felt the burning desire to write a book, now is the perfect time to embark on your authorial journey. In this article, we'll explore the excitement, challenges, and rewards that come with writing a book. So, are you ready to dive into the realm of words and create a masterpiece of your own?

Unleashing Your Creativity:
Writing a book is a powerful outlet for your creativity. It allows you to express your thoughts, emotions, and experiences in a way that resonates with readers. Whether you have a fictional tale brewing in your mind or a non-fiction book idea that can enlighten others, the act of writing enables you to let your imagination soar and bring your ideas to life.

Finding Your Writing Process:
Discovering your unique writing process is a crucial step in the journey of writing a book. Some authors thrive in organized environments, meticulously outlining their chapters and characters before diving into the writing process. Others prefer a more spontaneous approach, allowing the story to unfold naturally as they write. Experiment with different methods and find the writing process that best suits your style and fuels your creativity.

Overcoming Challenges:
Writing a book is not without its challenges. It requires discipline, dedication, and perseverance. Writer's block, self-doubt, and time management can all pose obstacles along the way. However, by adopting strategies such as setting writing goals, creating a writing routine, and seeking support from fellow writers or writing communities, you can overcome these challenges and keep your creative momentum flowing.

Writing is a powerful tool for communication, bridging gaps and connecting people across time and space. Whether you're sharing stories, ideas, or knowledge, writing allows you to convey your message with clarity and precision. Through your words, you can touch the hearts and minds of readers.

Crafting Memorable Characters and Engaging Plots:
One of the most thrilling aspects of writing a book is the opportunity to create memorable characters and captivating plots. Dive deep into character development, breathing life into your protagonists and antagonists. Craft a compelling plot that keeps readers turning pages, eager to unravel the twists and turns of your story. With each word, you have the power to transport readers to new worlds and evoke emotions that linger long after the final page.

Navigating the Publishing Landscape:
Once your manuscript is complete, the next step is to navigate the publishing landscape. Traditional publishing, self-publishing, and hybrid publishing are all viable options, each with its own advantages and considerations. Research the different paths, weigh the pros and cons, and choose the publishing route that aligns with your goals and aspirations as an author.

Sharing Your Book with the World:
Publishing your book is just the beginning. The joy of writing is in sharing your creation with the world. Engage in book launches, author readings, and literary events to connect with readers and build your author brand. Leverage the power of social media and online platforms to expand your reach and engage with a global audience. Embrace the feedback and reviews, as they provide valuable insights and fuel your growth as an author.

Embarking on the journey of writing a book is an exhilarating endeavor that opens doors to endless possibilities. It allows you to leave a lasting impact on readers, share your unique voice, and contribute to the rich tapestry of literature. So, are you ready to embrace your authorial journey? Grab your pen, unleash your creativity, and let the words flow onto the pages. Your book awaits, and the world is ready to be captivated by your story.

Sponsored by VMH Publishing
Visit: vmhpublishing.net

VMH
Publishing

At VMH Publishing, we believe in the transformative power of storytelling. We are a dedicated team of publishing professionals committed to empowering authors and inspiring readers through the written word. Our mission is to bring impactful stories to life, amplifying individual voices and creating connections that resonate with audiences.

Fashionable

BY VIKKI JONES

Immerse yourself in the meticulous craftsmanship behind each bag. Each bag is designed and manufactured with attention to detail, ensuring the highest quality.

www.vikkijones.com

Solitude on the Path to Goals

Written by Vikki Jones

As we navigate the tumultuous journey toward our goals, there often comes a time when we find ourselves standing at a crossroads, forced to leave behind the familiar comfort of companionship and venture into the solitary realm of our aspirations. It's a peculiar sensation, one that carries with it a tinge of guilt, particularly for those of us who have grown accustomed to extending a helping hand to others in their pursuits.

"It's a strange, guilty feeling, especially when I'm so accustomed to helping others with their businesses and ideas. Whether it's offering discounted rates when necessary, stretching myself thin, or passionately urging people to pursue their dreams with action, stepping into a realm where everything revolves around me is challenging. However, as the doors to my own dreams swing open, I must push through the guilt and the sense of leaving my friends, family, and associates behind. It's painful, but I won't run away," confesses one aspiring entrepreneur.

The path to success often demands a willingness to leave behind the safety net of familiar faces and supportive voices. It requires an individual to confront the discomfort of solitude and the quiet unease of forging ahead without the reassurance of companionship. This transition can be agonizing, as the very act of turning away from those who have stood by us feels like a betrayal of trust.

Yet, it is a testament to our determination and unwavering commitment to our dreams. As we step into the spotlight, we must find the strength to set aside the doubts and fears that threaten to hold us back. It is not a selfish act, but rather a necessary step in our personal evolution. We must acknowledge that our journey is uniquely our own, and while the path may be solitary, the destination holds the promise of fulfillment and accomplishment.

Leaving others behind is not an act of abandonment, but a declaration of our resolve to pursue our aspirations with unwavering dedication. It is a testament to our courage and resilience in the face of uncertainty. As we forge ahead, we carry with us the memories and lessons learned from those who have accompanied us thus far, drawing strength from their support as we navigate the uncharted terrain that lies ahead.

In the end, the bittersweet journey of leaving others behind is a poignant reminder of the sacrifices and challenges inherent in the pursuit of our dreams. It is a testament to the resilience of the human spirit, as we bravely embrace the solitude that accompanies our aspirations, knowing that it is a necessary step on the path to success.

Prioritize one's own growth and development.

Leaving others behind on the path to success can be seen as a sign of personal growth in several ways. Firstly, it demonstrates a willingness to prioritize one's own growth and development. When individuals recognize the need to focus on their own aspirations and take the necessary steps to pursue their goals, it reflects a level of self-awareness and a commitment to personal advancement.

Secondly, leaving others behind can signify the ability to set boundaries and make difficult decisions. It requires individuals to assess their relationships and understand that their journey may diverge from those of their friends, family, or colleagues. This process demands a level of emotional maturity and the capacity to make choices that align with one's own aspirations, even if they may cause temporary discomfort or disappointment to others.

Additionally, leaving others behind on the path to success can be a sign of courage and resilience. It often involves stepping out of one's comfort zone, venturing into the unknown, and embracing the solitude that comes with pursuing ambitious goals. This willingness to confront uncertainty and forge ahead despite potential resistance or disapproval from others reflects a strong sense of determination and inner strength.

Furthermore, it can be a sign of personal growth as it requires individuals to take ownership of their ambitions and responsibilities. By acknowledging that their journey is uniquely their own, individuals demonstrate a sense of accountability for their own success and well-being. This self-reliance and independence are essential aspects of personal growth and development.

Ultimately, leaving others behind on the path to success can be viewed as a sign of personal growth as it reflects self-awareness, the ability to set boundaries, courage, resilience, and a sense of accountability. While the decision to prioritize one's own aspirations may initially evoke feelings of guilt or discomfort, it is a crucial step in the journey towards personal fulfillment and achievement.

PRIORITIZE
SELF CARE
GUIDE & WORKBOOK

WRITTEN BY
VIKKI JONES